The Family *and Frog!* Haggadah

By Rabbi Ron Isaacs & Karen Rostoker-Gruber

Illustrations by Jackie Urbanovic

BEHRMAN HOUSE
www.behrmanhouse.com

For Bernie and Sol Scharfstein, groundbreaking pioneers
in the Jewish publishing industry. In gratitude for their
friendship and confidence in my work.
— RI

To all of our new family members, Aaron, Ethan, Ari, and Max.
~~Happy~~ Hoppy Passover!
— KR-G

For my niece, Josi, and her daughter,
Emanuelle, with love.
—JU

Text for the voice of Frog Copyright © 2017 KRG Entertainment, LLC
Text for the haggadah Copyright © 2017 Rabbi Ron, LLC
Illustrations Copyright © 2017 Behrman House, Inc.

Published by Behrman House, Inc.
Springfield, New Jersey 07081
www.behrmanhouse.com
ISBN 978-0-87441-937-5

Library of Congress Cataloging-in-Publication Data

Names: Isaacs, Ronald H., author. | Rostoker-Gruber, Karen, author. |
  Urbanovic, Jackie, illustrator.
Title: The Family (and Frog!) Haggadah / by Rabbi Ron Isaacs & Karen
  Rostoker-Gruber; illustrations by Jackie Urbanovic.
Description: Springfield, NJ: Behrman House, [2017] |
Identifiers: LCCN 2016019608 | ISBN 9780874419375 (alk. paper)
Subjects: LCSH: Haggadah--Adaptations--Juvenile literature. | Seder--Juvenile
  literature. | Passover--Prayers and devotions--Juvenile literature. |
  Jewish families--Prayers and devotions--Juvenile literature.
Classification: LCC BM674.795 .I83 2017 | DDC 296.4/5371--dc23 LC record available at
https://lccn.loc.gov/2016019608

Edited by Ann D. Koffsky
Book design by Terry Taylor

Printed in the United States of America

The publisher gratefully acknowledges the following sources of photographs and graphic images:
(T = Top; B = Bottom; M = Middle; L = Left; R = Right; 12a–n thumbnails p.12)
COVER: Shutterstock: Stevemart (frame); blueeyes (plate); Freddie Levin (Moses).
INTERIOR: Shutterstock: siro46 (parchment), Nella (flourishes, Arkady Mazor 4; ajt 4B, 15 (duck); Viktorija Reuta 5, 8, 13, 23, 44, 53, 55, 56 (crayon); David Orcea 12d, 12k, 17; 19, 26 (bear); Bildagentur Zoonar GmbH 5, 19, 20 (ball); Potapov Alexander 6 (feather); Garsya 6 (crumbs); janniwet 6, 27 (frame); Lichtmeister 6, 12, 14, 29, 30, 45 (page curl); david156 7T; Macrovector 7BR; blueeyes 8T, 8B; Zacarias Pereira da Mata 9BL; Aksenova Natalya 9R; Valentina Razumova 11 (flower); Igor Dudas 12R; Roman Dementyev 12a, 14M; tomertu 12g, 45MR, 45BL (matzah); vectorgirl 12m; aekky 13 (frame); Lane V. Erickson 16T; prapann 18, 35, 48 (frame); Africa Studio 19T, 20T (hole); stevemart 22 (frame); Kwitka 23BL, 44, 53B (arrow); Seamartini Graphics 26 (Letter O); Morphart Creation 28B; oriontrail 37 (frame); VladisChern 39, 49 (frame); Taigi 39B; gilya 41; sathaporn 44T (torn paper); Romiana Lee 46; Sean Pavone 47L; Tim UR 47R; Juango Tugores 50R; Yeryomina Anastassiya 50–51; pavelr 51T. Wikimedia Commons: Smooth.O 5B; British Library 6LM; Arthur Szyk 12e, 19, 22; Hadad Brothers 12f, 40; White House Flickr Account/Pete Souza 12j, 33TL; El Lissitzky 12n, 55; Anonymous Folk Artist 13T, 15T, 18; John Rose 23T; Jacob ben Judah Leib 23B; MNAC 26BR; James Tissot 26–27; Bible Illustrator 27L; the Providence Lithograph Company 28, 34; Internet Archive Book Images 29; Lidia Kozenitzky 30; Hortus Deliciarum 31B; Web Gallery of Art 35; The Jewish National and University Library 36T; Seforim 36B; Milwaukee Jewish Artist's Laboratory 37; Unknown 39T; Spc. Cassandra Monroe 44B; Unknown 48; Golden Haggadah 49B; Ji-Elle 53; Dr. Avishai Teicher Pikiwiki Israel 54. Other sources: Terry Taylor (frog footprints); Behrman House 9T, 12l, 49T; Gateways Haggadah/Rozensky 3, 10–11, 12b, 12c, 12h, 12i, 15LM, 16BR, 42T, 42B, 43; Israel Ministry of Tourism 13B; ©Rite Lite Judaica/ www.ritelite.com 21; Freddie Levin 31, 38 (Moses, hamsa); Ann D. Koffsky 32–33 (plagues).

Hibernating makes me hungry.

Introduction

Why is *The Family Haggadah* different *and Frog!* from all others?

At the seder, we gather to retell the story of the Exodus from Egypt and to enjoy a festive meal. Typically, seder participants follow the service in their own haggadah and use it as a guide to the Passover rituals. More than two thousand editions of the haggadah have been created over the years!

The Family Haggadah *and Frog!* gives you all that and so much more. There are lists to help you prepare and suggestions for activities to do during the seder, not to mention questions to ask and fascinating facts to read. There are also games to play and fun songs to sing.

All of these features are designed to help you have a great seder, at which each person experiences the feelings of the Exodus and the holiday of freedom.

And finally, a word about our star, Frog:

Vintage silver haggadah cover

I'm a star! Hold on. Let me get my crown.

You will find Frog popping (hopping?) up throughout this haggadah—which is what makes it different from any other. Why a frog, you ask? Because a frog is a unique animal, a symbol of transformation and change. It starts as a tadpole, with no feet and unable to breathe above water. As it grows, it transforms itself into an amphibious creature that can breathe freely on land and is also comfortable in the water.

Passover is about transformation, too. Its story tells of how an undistinguished group of Israelite slaves were transformed into a nation and found their way to freedom from slavery in the greatest empire of their time. So it is no coincidence that you'll find a friendly frog peeking through the pages.

We wish you a spirited and ~~riveting~~ ribitting seder experience.

Happy Passover!

Ron Isaacs
Karen Rostoker-Gruber . . . and Frog!

Searching for *Chameitz*

Before Passover starts, we clean our homes and get rid of all our bread, pasta, and most types of grains—also called *chameitz*. We do this to remember that when the Israelites fled Egypt, they left in such a hurry that the dough they had prepared for the journey did not have sufficient time to rise into bread. Instead, it became the flatbread that we call matzah.

Try This!

Make a *chameitz* scavenger hunt! On the night before Passover, place some pieces of bread around your home. Then, search for the *chameitz*. Use a candle or flashlight for light, and a feather and spoon to gather the bread into a paper bag.

Passover Cleaning from the *Golden Haggadah*, circa 1320

Wait! I found a piece of toadst!

Burning the *chameitz* in Safed, Israel

Burning the *Chameitz*

The next morning, dispose of the *chameitz* by burning it, paper bag and all, in a safe place. After the *chameitz* has started to burn, say:

Any leaven that may still be in my possession, which I have or have not seen, which I have or have not removed, shall be as if it does not exist and as ownerless as the dust of the earth.

If you find any flies in your search, let me know. I'll be more than hoppy to eat—I mean—throw them away for you.

Getting Ready

A Seder Checklist

Basics

☐ Wine or grape juice

☐ Candles

☐ Seder plate and its foods (see page 10)

☐ Three pieces of matzah, with a cover, on a plate

☐ Elijah's cup

☐ Frog's cup (filled with grape juice, please)

☐ Miriam's cup

☐ Pillow for each guest

☐ Bowl of salt water

☐ Cup, bowl, and towel for washing hands

☐ One haggadah for each person

☐ One wine cup for each person

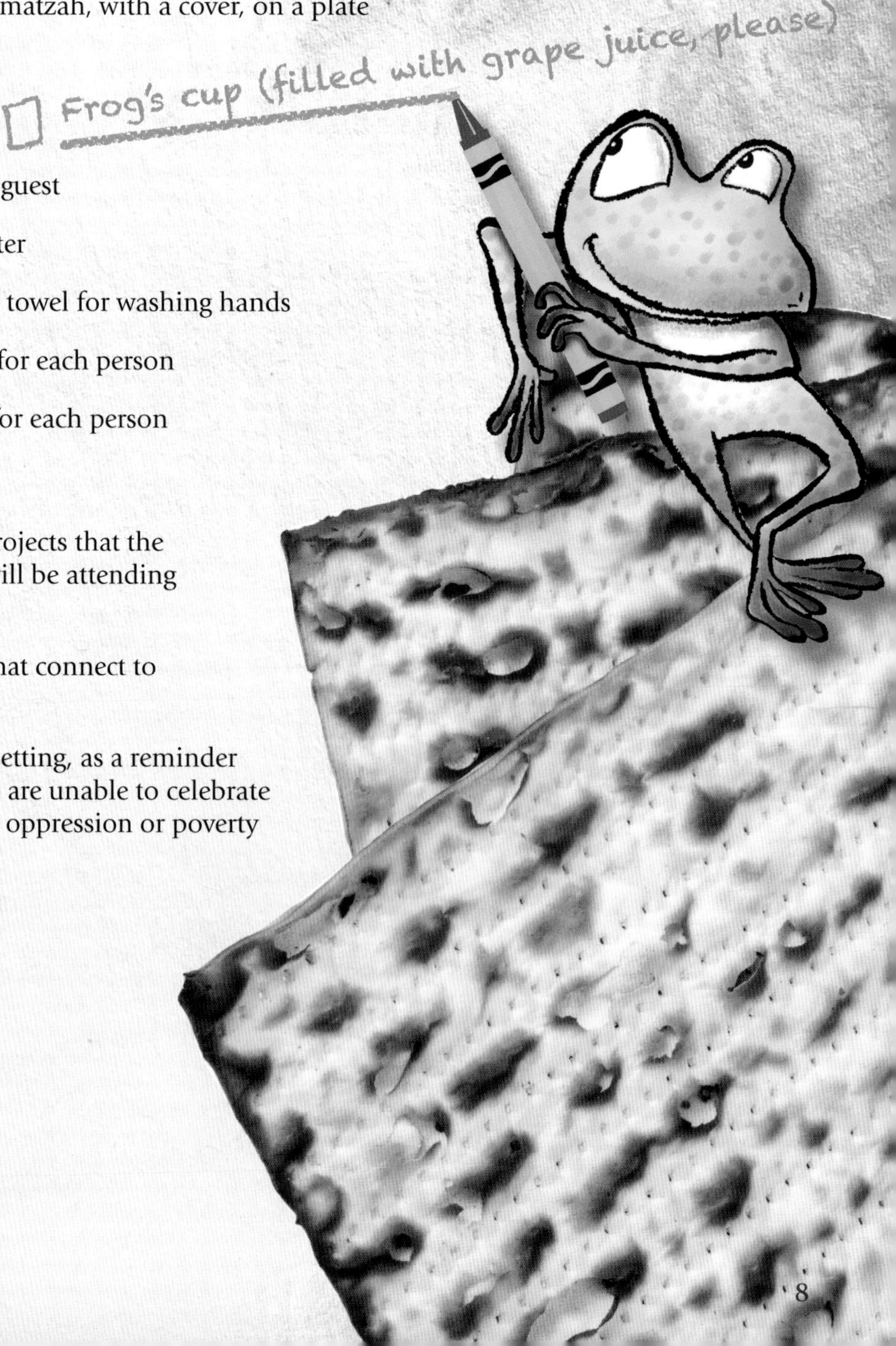

Extras

☐ Any Passover projects that the children who will be attending have made

☐ Toys or props that connect to the holiday

☐ An extra place setting, as a reminder of families who are unable to celebrate Passover due to oppression or poverty

Lighting the Candles

We begin the holiday with the lighting of candles.

Light the candles and recite the blessing below: (on Shabbat, add the words in parentheses).

בָּרוּךְ אַתָּה יְיָ אֱלֹהֵינוּ מֶלֶךְ הָעוֹלָם, אֲשֶׁר קִדְּשָׁנוּ בְּמִצְוֹתָיו וְצִוָּנוּ לְהַדְלִיק נֵר שֶׁל (שַׁבָּת וְשֶׁל) יוֹם טוֹב.

Baruch Atah Adonai Eloheinu Melech ha'olam, asher kid'shanu b'mitzvotav v'tzivanu l'hadlik neir shel (Shabbat v'shel) yom tov.

Praised are you, Adonai our God, Ruler of the universe, who makes us special through *mitzvot* and instructed us to light the (Shabbat and) festival candles.

Did you know?

The months and years of the Jewish calendar follow the cycles of the moon as it revolves around the Earth. Passover always starts when the moon is full.

Try This!

Go outside and look for the full moon.

9

The Seder Plate

All of the objects on the seder plate are symbols. They help us remember the Passover story and how Passover was celebrated in the times of the ancient Temple in Jerusalem:

Charoset חֲרוֹסֶת
A fruit and nut mixture usually including a combination of chopped apples, nuts, raisins, wine, and spices; a symbol of the mortar that the Jewish slaves would use as cement for the bricks.

Beitzah בֵּיצָה
A roasted egg (or an avocado for vegans); a symbol of the festival offering that was brought in the ancient Temple.

Karpas כַּרְפַּס
A vegetable, such as parsley; a reminder of spring.

Z'roa זְרוֹעַ
A roasted bone (or a roasted beet for vegetarians); a symbol of the Passover offering.

Maror מָרוֹר
A bitter herb, usually horseradish; a reminder of the bitterness of slavery.

Chazeret חֲזֶרֶת
A second variety of bitter vegetable such as romaine lettuce; a symbol of the bitterness of slave life.

Beitzah

Think About:

If you could add another symbol to the seder plate, what would it be? Why?

Order of the Seder

The word *seder* means "order." The Passover seder is made up of fourteen different rituals, all done in a particular order. Here is the *seder* of the seder.

 Kadeish: The blessing over wine or grape juice

 Ur'chatz: Washing hands

 Karpas: Dipping the vegetable in salt water and eating it

 Yachatz: Breaking the middle matzah

 Magid: Telling the Passover Story

 Rochtzah: Washing hands

 Motzi Matzah: Eating matzah

 Maror: Eating the bitter herbs

 Koreich: Eating the Hillel sandwich

 Shulchan Oreich: The festive meal

 Tzafun: Eating the *afikoman*

 Bareich: Giving thanks for the meal

 Hallel: Singing songs of praise

 Nirtzah: Completing the seder

Try This!

Sing the names of the steps of the seder in Hebrew to the tune of "On Top of Old Smokey."

Hey, can we change the seder of the seder and sing first? I brought my guitar.

Celebrating Passover,
Russia, 18th century

Think About:

Ask everyone to finish these sentences:

At this seder, I expect...

At this seder, I hope to have fun by...

I can make this seder meaningful to me by...

toadily awesome

No one filled my cup.

Kadeish
Blessing the Wine or Grape Juice

Tonight we will drink four cups of wine or grape juice, one for each of the four promises of freedom that God made to our Israelite ancestors in Egypt.

Raise the first cup of wine or grape juice and read together the first of the four promises:

"I am God, and I will free you from slavery in Egypt." (Exodus 6:6)

Say the blessings below:

בָּרוּךְ אַתָּה יְיָ אֱלֹהֵינוּ מֶלֶךְ הָעוֹלָם, בּוֹרֵא פְּרִי הַגָּפֶן.

Baruch Atah Adonai Eloheinu Melech ha'olam, borei p'ri hagafen.

Praised are You, Adonai our God, Ruler of the universe, who creates the fruit of the vine.

בָּרוּךְ אַתָּה יְיָ אֱלֹהֵינוּ מֶלֶךְ הָעוֹלָם, שֶׁהֶחֱיָנוּ וְקִיְּמָנוּ וְהִגִּיעָנוּ לַזְּמַן הַזֶּה.

Baruch Atah Adonai Eloheinu Melech ha'olam, shehecheyanu, v'kiy'manu, v'higi'anu laz'man hazeh.

Praised are You, Adonai our God, Ruler of the universe, who has given us life, sustained us, and brought us to this moment.

Drink from the first cup of wine or grape juice while reclining to the left.

Ur'chatz

Washing Our Hands

Since the seder is a sacred meal, we wash our hands to get ourselves ready for it.

Using a pitcher or cup, pour water over each hand, either at the sink or at the table with a bowl to catch the water. (No blessing is said at this time.)

Did you know?

There are unique table manners tonight: you're free to sit in whatever way is most comfortable for you! Some even place soft pillows on their chairs for extra comfort.

Game Time

See who can guess what the letters below stand for first! (answers on page 56)

MC   4 Q   8 D of P
4 C of W   10 P   H S
F C

Did someone say "wash"?

Karpas

Dipping the Greens

Spring is the time of rebirth, when plants and animals seem to come alive again after being asleep all winter. By dipping the springtime vegetable into salt water, we remember the salty tears of our enslaved ancestors, together with the hope of spring.

Take the green vegetable and dip it in salt water.

Say the blessing:

בָּרוּךְ אַתָּה יְיָ אֱלֹהֵינוּ מֶלֶךְ הָעוֹלָם, בּוֹרֵא פְּרִי הָאֲדָמָה.

Baruch Atah Adonai Eloheinu Melech ha'olam, borei p'ri ha'adamah.

Praised are You, Adonai our God, Ruler of the universe, who creates the fruit of the earth.

Eat the *karpas*.

Try This!

Serve *karpas* appetizers (carrots, boiled potatoes, celery, parsnips, pickles), so that those who are already hungry can eat something before the main meal.

Which piece is just right?

Did you know?

Moroccan Jews traditionally eat a piece of the afikoman and save the rest as a good luck charm for protecting them in their travels.

Yachatz

Breaking the Middle Matzah

We now break the middle matzah into two pieces. We will use the bigger portion for the *afikoman*, which we will eat as dessert. The smaller portion will be eaten along with the first matzah when we say the special blessing at the beginning of the meal.

Uncover the three matzahs. Hold up the middle one for everyone to see, and break it in two. Put the smaller piece back with the other two, and hide the larger piece for the *afikoman*.

Can you make me a piece shaped like a lily pad?

Try This!

Jewish mystics break the middle matzah into the shape of the Hebrew letters *dalet* (symbolizing the number 4) and *vav* (symbolizing the number 6), equaling the ten attributes of God. See if you can do it!

The Ha Lachma Anya prayer, as depicted in the *Barcelona Haggadah*, 14th century

Try This!

Add one more matzah to the pile, and name it the "Matzah of Hope." Announce that it is a symbol of all Jews throughout the world who are not able to celebrate a Passover seder.

Magid

Telling the Story

Before we begin telling the Passover story, we first bring to mind those who are less fortunate and invite "all who are hungry to come and eat."

Uncover the matzah, raise it high, and say:

הָא לַחְמָא עַנְיָא דִי אֲכָלוּ אַבְהָתָנָא בְּאַרְעָא דְמִצְרָיִם.

Ha lachma anya di achalu avhatana b'ara d'Mitzrayim.

This is the bread of poverty that our ancestors ate in the Land of Egypt. Let all who are hungry come join us for the meal. Now we are here; next year, may we be in the Land of Israel. Now we are still slaves; next year, may we be truly free.

Fill the second cup of wine or grape juice.

So, why do we ask the Four Questions? That's a good question!

Being able to ask questions and have them answered is a sign of freedom, so telling the story of Passover through questions and answers emphasizes that we are a free people.

The Four Questions, by Arthur Szyk, 1940

Is it too late for me to ask the Four Questions?

Think About:

Why do you think we ask the same four questions every year?

The Four Questions

The youngest person asks or sings the Four Questions:

מַה נִּשְׁתַּנָּה הַלַּיְלָה הַזֶּה מִכָּל הַלֵּילוֹת?

1. שֶׁבְּכָל הַלֵּילוֹת אָנוּ אוֹכְלִין חָמֵץ וּמַצָּה. הַלַּיְלָה הַזֶּה כֻּלּוֹ מַצָּה.

2. שֶׁבְּכָל הַלֵּילוֹת אָנוּ אוֹכְלִין שְׁאָר יְרָקוֹת. הַלַּיְלָה הַזֶּה מָרוֹר.

3. שֶׁבְּכָל הַלֵּילוֹת אֵין אָנוּ מַטְבִּילִין אֲפִילוּ פַּעַם אֶחָת. הַלַּיְלָה הַזֶּה שְׁתֵּי פְעָמִים.

4. שֶׁבְּכָל הַלֵּילוֹת אָנוּ אוֹכְלִין בֵּין יוֹשְׁבִין וּבֵין מְסֻבִּין. הַלַּיְלָה הַזֶּה כֻּלָּנוּ מְסֻבִּין.

Mah nishtanah halailah hazeh mikol haleilot?

1. *Sheb'chol haleilot anu och'lin chameitz umatzah. Halailah hazeh kulo matzah.*

2. *Sheb'chol haleilot anu och'lin sh'ar y'rakot. Halailah hazeh maror.*

3. *Sheb'chol haleilot ein anu matbilin afilu pa'am echat. Halailah hazeh sh'tei f'amim.*

4. *Sheb'chol haleilot anu och'lin bein yoshvin uvein m'subin. Halailah hazeh kulanu m'subin.*

How is this night different from all other nights?

1. On all other nights we eat either *chameitz* or matzah. On this night, we eat only matzah.

2. On all other nights we eat all kinds of vegetables. On this night, we eat bitter herbs.

3. On all other nights we usually don't dip our vegetables even once. On this night we dip twice.

4. On all other nights we eat either sitting straight or sitting in a relaxed position. On this night we all eat in a relaxed position.

The Four Questions
finger puppets

Avadim Hayinu: We Were Slaves

We continue telling the Passover story by reminding ourselves that once we were slaves.

Say or sing:

עֲבָדִים הָיִינוּ, הָיִינוּ, עַתָּה
בְּנֵי־חוֹרִין, בְּנֵי־חוֹרִין.

Avadim hayinu, hayinu. Atah b'nei chorin, b'nei chorin.

We were slaves to Pharaoh in Egypt, but God brought us out with a mighty hand and an outstretched arm. Had God not brought us out of Egypt we would still be slaves to Pharaoh— and so would our children and grandchildren.

Think About:

What do you think would be the worst thing about being a slave?

Did you know?

One of the longest seders ever recorded is the seder of the five rabbis of B'nei B'rak. Rabbi Eliezer, Rabbi Yehoshua, Rabbi Elazar ben Azaryah, Rabbi Akiva, and Rabbi Tarfon spent the entire night telling the story of the Exodus.

Let's not do this one, OK?

The Rabbis of B'nei B'rak by Judah ben Judah Leib

Slaves dancing on a South Carolina plantation, 1785

"Let My People Go" (an African American spiritual):

When Israel was in Egypt's land,

Let my people go.

Oppressed so hard they could not stand,

Let my people go.

Go down, Moses, way down in Egypt land.

Tell old Pharaoh,

"Let my people go."

23

The Four Children

Each of us is really good at some things and not so good at others. Our sages recognized this. They knew that each of us understands things in different ways, and each of us learns differently. To reflect this understanding, they chose to describe four different children. Perhaps they were saying that each of us has a bit of those four personality types within us. Depending on where we are and how we feel—whether we feel calm or angry, smart or not—different parts of those four children come out.

Read aloud the passages about the four children:

❧ *The Wise Child* ❧

What does the wise child ask? "What are the specific things that God asked us to do?" We tell this child all of the laws and customs of Passover.

❧ *The Defiant Child* ❧

What does the defiant child ask? "What does this seder have to do with you?" This child chooses to reject our community and abandon a relationship with the Jewish people. We challenge this child, saying that we celebrate Passover because God took our people out of slavery. But since you set yourself apart from our people, you would not have been freed.

The Uncomplicated Child

What does the uncomplicated child ask? "What happened? Can you tell me the story?" We gently reply, "With a mighty hand, God brought us out of Egypt and a life of slavery."

The Child Who Does Not Know How to Ask

This child does not understand that something unique and unusual is going on. We capture this child's interest and explain that Passover reminds us of what God did for us when we were freed from slavery in Egypt.

Think About:

Describe a time when you were unable to think of a question to ask. How did you feel? What did you do?

Think back to the cleverest question you were ever asked. What was it, and how did you respond to it?

I like stories.

The Passover Story

This story, about how the Israelites became a free people, is the heart of the haggadah. In fact, the word *haggadah* comes from the same root as *magid*, which is the Hebrew term for "storytelling."

So let's get to the story:

Once upon a time...

In ancient times, our ancestors worshipped idols, until one man, Abraham, came to worship one God. Abraham and his wife, Sara, dwelled in Canaan and taught the word of God to people throughout the land. God blessed them, and they had a child, Isaac, and grandchildren, Jacob and Esau. Jacob, who later became known as Israel, went down to live in Egypt with his family.

Why did our ancestor Jacob move his family to Egypt? Jacob's son, Joseph, had become the prime minister of Egypt. He was the most powerful man in the land, second only to Pharaoh, the king. Joseph was a wise and just leader who made sure that the Egyptian people prospered and were also prepared against calamity. So when a terrible famine arose in Canaan and in Egypt, the Egyptians were well fed and thriving, while the people of Canaan were not so fortunate. Jacob's family was at great risk of starvation, so Joseph invited them to come and live in Egypt, where they would be safe. And thus our ancestors moved to Egypt, where they lived in peace for generations.

Abraham by Juan Gascó, circa 1500

26

Did you see that? Yum! I think it's a fly.

Finding of Moses, 1926

But soon, a new king arose over Egypt who didn't remember the good that Joseph had done. This Pharaoh feared the Israelites, as our ancestors were called. He refused to recognize their contributions to Egyptian society and instead saw their growth, prosperity, and great numbers as a threat. So he made them his slaves. Surely, he thought, the humiliation and hard labor of slavery would break their spirit, and their numbers would be depleted. He would no longer need to be afraid of them.

But instead, the Israelites kept their faith and held fast to their ways. They grew and had families. Frustrated that his plan had failed, and fearful that the numerous Israelites would overthrow him someday, Pharaoh was determined to destroy our people. He decreed that all Israelite baby boys be drowned in the Nile River.

One Israelite woman, Yocheved, hid her baby son to keep him alive. She placed him in a basket alongside the Nile River and sent his sister, Miriam, to watch over him. One day, while bathing in the Nile, Pharaoh's daughter found the basket. When she opened it and saw the baby, her heart filled with compassion. She chose to defy her own father's edict that the baby be killed, and she adopted the child. She named him Moses, which means "drawn from the water."

Moses grew up in the luxury of Pharaoh's palace. But

Joseph and His Bretheren Welcomed by Pharaoh by James Tissot

he could not ignore the suffering of his people, and our tradition teaches that he would often intervene and help whenever he saw a slave struggling with a heavy, crushing load. One day he saw an Egyptian beating an Israelite slave, and he stepped in to defend the slave. In his anger, Moses killed the Egyptian. Fearing for his life, Moses fled from Egypt and settled in the land of Midian. There he married Zipporah and became a shepherd.

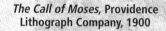

The Call of Moses, Providence Lithograph Company, 1900

One day, Moses came upon a bush that, to his amazement, burned without being consumed. Then God spoke to Moses from the bush, saying, "I am the God of your ancestors, and I have seen the suffering of my people." God commanded Moses to return to Egypt and lead the Israelites to freedom.

So Moses and his brother, Aaron, went to Pharaoh

spoke to Moses

and demanded that he free the Israelites. But Pharaoh hardened his heart and refused. In punishment for Pharaoh's refusal, God brought terrible plagues upon the land—blood, frogs, lice, wild beasts, cattle disease, boils, hail, locusts, and darkness. Though his people suffered from these plagues, Pharaoh remained defiant and would not let our ancestors go out from his land.

Then came the tenth and most terrible plague. Every firstborn Egyptian died. Only the Israelites were spared. A great cry rose up from Egypt, and Pharaoh's will was finally broken. He agreed to let the Israelites go free.

Moses and Aaron before Pharaoh, 1896

Blech! That was a locust!

The Israelites left in a great hurry. Soon after, Pharaoh regretted his decision and sent his army to recapture the Israelites and bring them back to slavery. His army pursued our people and trapped them at the Sea of Reeds.

With the army at their backs and the sea before them, they had no chance of escape. But God told Moses to raise his staff, and, miraculously, the waters parted, allowing the Israelites to cross through.

When the Egyptian army chased after them, the waters closed in, drowning the Egyptians. Safely on the other side, Moses and his sister, Miriam, led the people in joyous song and dance in praise of God.

Splitting of the Red Sea
by Dr. Lidia Kozenitzky

Can you feel that? The ground is shaking! It's Pharaoh's soldiers!! Run!!!

And so began the Israelites' journey from slavery to freedom, from sadness to joy, from being strangers in Egypt to becoming a great nation.

Say or sing:

וְהִיא שֶׁעָמְדָה לַאֲבוֹתֵינוּ וְלָנוּ.

V'hi she'amdah la'avoteinu v'lanu.

In every generation enemies have risen up against us, and God has saved us from their hands.

Crossing of the Red Sea from the *Hortus Deliciarum*

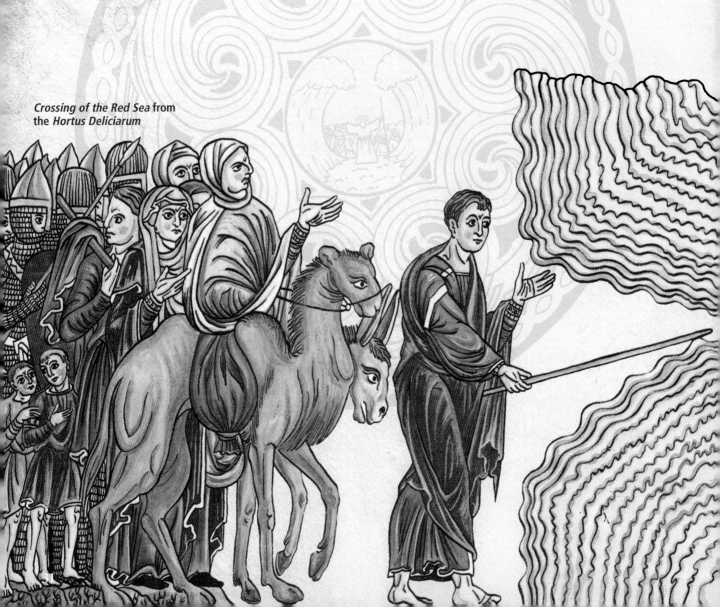

The Ten Plagues

God heard the cries of the Israelites, who were suffering under the Egyptians' terrible oppression, and brought ten terrible plagues to Egypt to convince Pharaoh to free our ancestors.

Yet, despite the many cruel actions of the ancient Egyptians, we still choose to have compassion for them. We remove a drop of wine or juice from our cups each time we say the name of a plague to remember that while the plagues resulted in our freedom, they caused the ancient Egyptians suffering, and our joy is lessened.

Recite the names of the plagues aloud. Each time the name of a plague is said, remove a drop of wine or grape juice from your cup.

Think About:

Go around the table and ask people to share what they think is a modern-day plague that has created a problem for the world.

kinim lice

כִּנִּים

tz'fardei'a frogs

צְפַרְדֵּעַ

dam blood

דָּם

arbeh locusts

אַרְבֶּה

barad hail

בָּרָד

sh'chin boils

שְׁחִין

32

Reciting the ten plagues at the White House seder, 2016

Who let the plagues out?
Who? Who? Who?
Who let the plagues out?
Who? Who? Who?

dever cattle disease
דֶּבֶר

arov wild beasts
עָרוֹב

Game Time

Try a game of reverse charades. Choose a plague and have everyone at the seder except for one person act it out without using words. The one person tries to guess the name of the plague.

makat b'chorot
slaying of the firstborn
מַכַּת בְּכוֹרוֹת

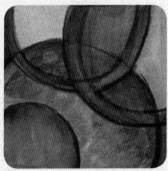

choshech darkness
חֹשֶׁךְ

Dayeinu: It Would Have Been Enough

The song "Dayeinu" expresses thanks to God for everything God did for us during and after the Exodus from Egypt. The chorus says it all: *Dayeinu*—it would have been enough!

Sing together:

Ilu hotzi'anu miMitzrayim—dayeinu!

אִלּוּ הוֹצִיאָנוּ מִמִּצְרַיִם, דַּיֵּנוּ.

Had God only taken us out of Egypt—*dayeinu!*

Ilu natan lanu et haShabbat—dayeinu!

אִלּוּ נָתַן לָנוּ אֶת הַשַּׁבָּת, דַּיֵּנוּ.

Had God only given us Shabbat—*dayeinu!*

Ilu natan lanu et haTorah—dayeinu!

אִלּוּ נָתַן לָנוּ אֶת הַתּוֹרָה, דַּיֵּנוּ.

Had God only given us the Torah—*dayeinu!*

Think About:

Complete these sentences:

It is not enough for us only to eat matzah. We must also...

It is not enough to be upset with the fighting in the world. We must also...

It is not enough to recite "Let all who are hungry come and eat." We must also...

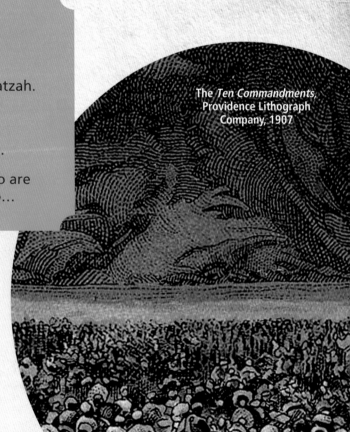

The *Ten Commandments*, Providence Lithograph Company, 1907

After the leader recites each verse below, everyone responds "Dayeinu"

Had God only brought us out of Egypt and not divided the sea for us—*dayeinu!*

Had God only divided the sea for us and not led us through on dry land—*dayeinu!*

Had God only led us through on dry land and not cared for us in the desert for forty years—*dayeinu!*

Had God only cared for us in the desert for forty years and not brought us to the land of Israel—*dayeinu!*

The *Feast of Passover* by Dieric Bouts, circa 1460

I have an idea. Let's "pass over" this part of the seder and eat!

Pesach, Matzah, Maror

Many believe that the three most important symbols at the seder are the *pesach* (shank bone), the matzah, and the *maror*.

Pesach

The *pesach* symbolizes the Paschal lamb—the Passover offering—and is represented by the roasted bone or beet. It reminds us of the Passover sacrifice that our ancestors brought to the Jerusalem Temple to celebrate the Exodus from Egypt. It is called *pesach*, which means "pass over," because God passed over the Israelites and only harmed the firstborn Egyptians.

Matzah

This matzah reminds us of how the Israelites left Egypt in such a hurry that they did not have time for their dough to rise and become bread.

Maror

This *maror* reminds us of how the Egyptians made the lives of the Israelites bitter with hard and punishing work.

Think About:

If you could choose the three most important symbols for the seder, what would they be?

Did you know?

The historic Jewish involvement in human rights is an outgrowth of this three-thousand-year-old reminder that we ourselves were once slaves.

In Every Generation

In every generation, even today when we are blessed to live in freedom, each of us should feel as though we personally were a part of the Exodus from Egypt.

בְּכָל דּוֹר וָדוֹר חַיָּב אָדָם לִרְאוֹת אֶת עַצְמוֹ
כְּאִלּוּ הוּא יָצָא מִמִּצְרַיִם.

B'chol dor vador chayav adam lirot et atzmo k'ilu hu yatza miMitzrayim.

In every generation, each of us must look upon ourselves as if we personally were freed from Egypt.

Try This!

Take turns passing around a mirror, and have participants look into it and visualize themselves as a slave.

Mirror, mirror, in my hand.
I want freedom in this land!

Fifth Zionist Congress Souvenir by Ephraim Lilien, 1901

Halleluyah: Praise God

Filled with gratitude, we recite psalms to thank
God for all the good things that God has done for us.

Everyone raises their cups and says the following together:

It is our duty to give thanks, sing praises, and offer
blessings to God who did these miracles for our
ancestors and for us. For bringing us:

from slavery to freedom,

from sadness to joy,

from darkness to light.

Therefore, let us sing a new song, *Halleluyah!*

בְּצֵאת יִשְׂרָאֵל מִמִּצְרָיִם,
בֵּית יַעֲקֹב מֵעַם לֹעֵז.
הָיְתָה יְהוּדָה לְקָדְשׁוֹ,
יִשְׂרָאֵל מַמְשְׁלוֹתָיו.
הַיָּם רָאָה וַיָּנֹס, הַיַּרְדֵּן יִסֹּב לְאָחוֹר.

B'tzeit Yisrael miMitzrayim,

beit Ya'akov, mei'am lo'eiz.

Haitah Y'hudah l'kodsho,

Yisrael mamsh'lotav.

Hayam ra'ah vayanos, haYardein yisov l'achor.

When Israel came forth out of Egypt,

The house of Jacob from a people of strange language,

Judah became God's sanctuary,

Israel God's dominion.

The sea saw it and fled; the Jordan turned backward.

(Psalms 114)

Matzah from the *Barcelona Haggadah*, 14th century

Yay! More grape juice!!!

The Second Cup

Raise the second cup of wine or grape juice and read together the second of the four promises:

"I will deliver you from slavery." (Exodus 6:6)

Say the blessing:

בָּרוּךְ אַתָּה יְיָ אֱלֹהֵינוּ מֶלֶךְ הָעוֹלָם, בּוֹרֵא פְּרִי הַגָּפֶן.

Baruch Atah Adonai Eloheinu Melech ha'olam, borei p'ri hagafen.

Praised are You, Adonai our God, Ruler of the universe, who creates the fruit of the vine.

Drink from the second cup of wine or grape juice.

39

Rochtzah
Washing Our Hands

The seder is no ordinary meal. It is filled with ritual, questioning, telling, singing, and, of course, eating! In Jewish tradition eating is seen as a holy act; in fact, the ancient rabbis compared the dinner table to the altar in the Temple. We wash our hands, as the priests did, to elevate the ordinary act of eating into one that is extraordinary and sacred.

Using a pitcher or cup, pour water over each hand, either at the sink or at the table with a bowl to catch the water, and then recite the blessing:

בָּרוּךְ אַתָּה יְיָ אֱלֹהֵינוּ מֶלֶךְ הָעוֹלָם, אֲשֶׁר קִדְּשָׁנוּ בְּמִצְוֹתָיו וְצִוָּנוּ עַל נְטִילַת יָדָיִם.

Baruch Atah Adonai Eloheinu Melech ha'olam, asher kid'shanu b'mitzvotav v'tzivanu al n'tilat yadayim.

Praised are You, Adonai our God, Ruler of the universe, who makes us special through *mitzvot* and instructed us to wash our hands.

Silver washing cup

I heard someone say "wash" again.

Think About:

What are some other things that you can do just before or during a meal to add meaning?

40

Motzi Matzah
Eating the Matzah

Since we are about to eat the matzah, we take the opportunity to say two blessings of thanks. The first expresses appreciation for all kinds of breads, and the second for matzah.

The leader distributes pieces of the top and middle matzah to each person.

Say the two blessings as a group, and eat the matzah.

בָּרוּךְ אַתָּה יְיָ אֱלֹהֵינוּ מֶלֶךְ הָעוֹלָם, הַמּוֹצִיא לֶחֶם מִן הָאָרֶץ.

Baruch Atah Adonai Eloheinu Melech ha'olam, hamotzi lechem min ha'aretz.

Praised are You, Adonai our God, Ruler of the universe, who brings forth bread from the earth.

בָּרוּךְ אַתָּה יְיָ אֱלֹהֵינוּ מֶלֶךְ הָעוֹלָם, אֲשֶׁר קִדְּשָׁנוּ בְּמִצְוֹתָיו וְצִוָּנוּ
עַל אֲכִילַת מַצָּה.

Baruch Atah Adonai Eloheinu Melech ha'olam, asher kid'shanu b'mitzvotav v'tzivanu al achilat matzah.

Praised are You, Adonai our God, Ruler of the universe, who makes us special through *mitzvot* and instructed us to eat matzah.

Think About:

During the time of the Talmud, matzah was made with designs on it, including pictures of doves, fish, and flowers. If you could design a matzah, what picture would you add to it?

I made a matzah mess.

Maror
Eating the Bitter Herbs

The bitter *maror* reminds us of the pain our ancestors felt as slaves in Egypt, and the *charoset* we dip it into looks like the mortar they used for cementing the bricks.

Say the blessing and eat the *maror* dipped in *charoset*.

בָּרוּךְ אַתָּה יְיָ אֱלֹהֵינוּ מֶלֶךְ הָעוֹלָם, אֲשֶׁר קִדְּשָׁנוּ בְּמִצְוֹתָיו וְצִוָּנוּ עַל אֲכִילַת מָרוֹר.

Baruch Atah Adonai Eloheinu Melech ha'olam, asher kid'shanu b'mitzvotav v'tzivanu al achilat maror.

Praised are You, Adonai our God, Ruler of the universe, who makes us special through *mitzvot* and instructed us to eat *maror*.

Koreich
Making Hillel's Sandwich

In Temple times, the famous Rabbi Hillel made a sandwich with matzah, meat from the Passover offering, and *maror*. Why? So he could eat all of the ingredients of the bitterness of slavery together and fulfill the biblical verse, "With *matzot* and bitter herbs they shall eat it [the Passover offering]" (Exodus 12:8), in one bite.

Today, we follow Rabbi Hillel's example and make our own Hillel sandwiches. But since we no longer bring sacrifices, our ingredients include the matzah, *maror*, and *charoset*.

Distribute pieces of the top and middle matzah to each person.

Did you know?

The fourth Earl of Sandwich, who lived in the eighteenth century, is usually considered the inventor of the sandwich. But Hillel's sandwich came first!

"Take Me Out to the Seder"

Take me out to the seder.

Take me out to the crowd.

So much fun, and it's now time to eat,

and eat, and eat, and eat, eat, eat, eat!

For we'll root, root, root for the Israelites

As they will soon be set free

For it's one, two, three—four cups of wine

Let's now eat and drink merrily.

Try This!

Since we are getting close to the meal, now is a good time to stretch our legs and arms (just like at a baseball game in the seventh inning) and sing!

Throw me a matzah ball! Come on! I'm ready!

Service members
celebrate Passover

Shulchan Oreich
Serving the Meal

Many families serve hard-boiled eggs at the beginning of the meal, because they are a symbol of spring, renewal, and the new life that the Israelites enjoyed after being liberated from Egypt. Some say that we use hard-boiled eggs because the more you boil an egg, the harder it gets, just as the Israelites became stronger (more numerous) the more that Pharaoh punished them. Other traditional dishes can include chicken soup, brisket, gefilte fish, and more. Enjoy the delicious meal!

I hope there's a fly in my soup.

I'm not telling you the answers. You have to check page 56.

Game Time
Can you unscramble the Passover words below?

GUALPE   TYPGE   EFMDORE

TAZHMA   CLOTSUS

SUFPRCGO

Tzafun
Eating the Afikoman

For dessert, we eat the *afikoman*, so that the taste of matzah is the last thing we take away from the seder. But first, we have to find it!

Some ideas: Have the *afikoman* hider sing a song (the "Dayeinu" chorus works well) while the searchers are looking—louder as the searchers approach the hiding place and softer as they get farther from it.

When the *akfikoman* is found, distribute a piece of the matzah to each participant to eat.

Did you know?

During the Middle Ages, *matzahs* were made very thick (even thicker than a bagel) and circular in shape.

I'm going to find you, Afikoman, if it's the last thing I do!

Bareich
Giving Thanks

After the meal we thank God for all of the gifts from God that we have received. These include the gift of having friends, family, and ample food to eat. We end by asking God to help bring peace to Israel and the entire world.

Fill the third cup of wine or grape juice. Say or sing the blessings:

בָּרוּךְ אַתָּה יְיָ אֱלֹהֵינוּ מֶלֶךְ הָעוֹלָם, הַזָּן אֶת הָעוֹלָם כֻּלּוֹ בְּטוּבוֹ בְּחֵן בְּחֶסֶד וּבְרַחֲמִים. הוּא נוֹתֵן לֶחֶם לְכָל בָּשָׂר כִּי לְעוֹלָם חַסְדּוֹ. וּבְטוּבוֹ הַגָּדוֹל תָּמִיד לֹא חָסַר לָנוּ, וְאַל יֶחְסַר לָנוּ מָזוֹן לְעוֹלָם וָעֶד בַּעֲבוּר שְׁמוֹ הַגָּדוֹל, כִּי הוּא אֵל זָן וּמְפַרְנֵס לַכֹּל וּמֵטִיב לַכֹּל, וּמֵכִין מָזוֹן לְכָל בְּרִיּוֹתָיו אֲשֶׁר בָּרָא. בָּרוּךְ אַתָּה, יְיָ, הַזָּן אֶת הַכֹּל.

Baruch Atah Adonai Eloheinu Melech ha'olam, hazan et ha'olam kulo b'tuvo b'chein b'chesed uv'rachamim. Hu notein lechem l'chol basar ki l'olam chasdo. Uv'tuvo hagadol tamid lo chaser lanu, v'al yechsar lanu mazon l'olam va'ed ba'avur sh'mo hagadol, ki hu El zan um'farneis lakol umeitiv lakol, umeichin mazon l'chol b'riyotav asher bara. Baruch Atah, Adonai, hazan et hakol.

Praised are You, Adonai our God, Ruler of the universe, who nourishes the whole world with goodness and grace, kindness and mercy. You provide for all. Your goodness has caused us never to want for food. You prepare food for all creatures and bring goodness to all. Praised are You, Adonai, Provider for all.

Think About:

There are lots of hungry people in the world who have very little for which to say thanks. What are some things you can do to help?

The Third Cup

Raise the third cup of wine or grape juice and read together the third of the four promises:

"I will save you with an outstretched arm and great judgments." (Exodus 6:6)

Say the blessing:

בָּרוּךְ אַתָּה יְיָ אֱלֹהֵינוּ מֶלֶךְ הָעוֹלָם, בּוֹרֵא פְּרִי הַגָּפֶן.

Baruch Atah Adonai Eloheinu Melech ha'olam, borei p'ri hagafen.

Praised are You, Adonai our God, Ruler of the universe, who creates the fruit of the vine.

Drink from the third cup of wine or grape juice.

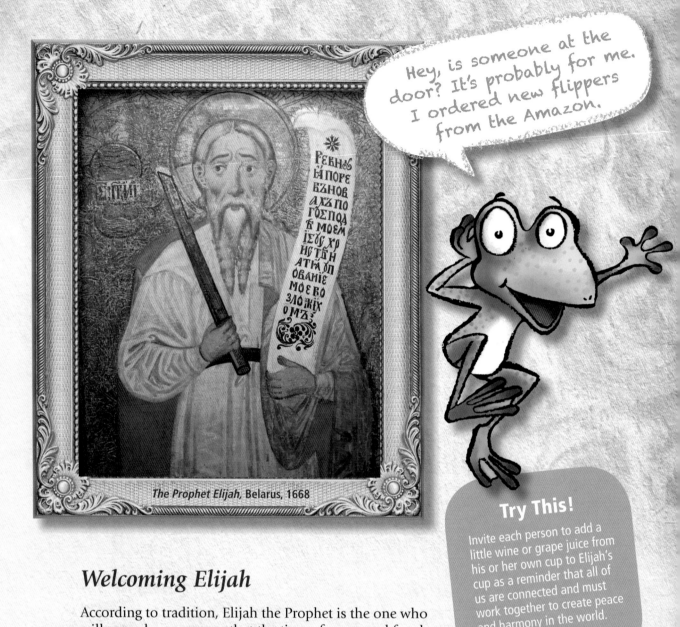

The Prophet Elijah, Belarus, 1668

Hey, is someone at the door? It's probably for me. I ordered new flippers from the Amazon.

Try This!

Invite each person to add a little wine or grape juice from his or her own cup to Elijah's cup as a reminder that all of us are connected and must work together to create peace and harmony in the world.

Welcoming Elijah

According to tradition, Elijah the Prophet is the one who will someday announce that the time of peace and freedom has arrived. We set out a special cup of wine for him, called Elijah's cup.

Ask a child to open the door of your home to welcome Elijah, and sing:

אֵלִיָּהוּ הַנָּבִיא, אֵלִיָּהוּ הַתִּשְׁבִּי, אֵלִיָּהוּ, אֵלִיָּהוּ, אֵלִיָּהוּ הַגִּלְעָדִי,

בִּמְהֵרָה בְיָמֵינוּ יָבֹא אֵלֵינוּ עִם מָשִׁיחַ בֶּן דָּוִד.

Eliyahu hanavi, Eliyahu haTishbi, Eliyahu, Eliyahu, Eliyahu haGiladi. Bimheirah v'yameinu yavo eileinu, im Mashiach ben David.

Elijah the prophet, Elijah the Tishbite, Elijah, Elijah, Elijah from Gilead, quickly in our days may he come to us with the Messiah, son of David.

Honoring Miriam

We set aside a cup filled with water to honor Miriam the prophet. The water is a reminder of the miraculous well that, according to tradition, provided the Israelites with fresh water in the desert because of Miriam's merit.

There is a custom in some homes of having participants at the seder each pour water from their own glasses into Miriam's cup and then recite: "This is Miriam's cup, the cup of living water."

Did you know?

The first documented seder that included Miriam's cup took place in Boston, in 1989. The new ritual was developed as a way to celebrate and highlight the role of women in the Exodus story and throughout Jewish history.

Miriam from the *Golden Haggadah,* circa 1320

Hallel
Psalms of Praise

We now sing psalms of praise to show our gratitude for the many things that God has done for the Jewish people.

Fill the fourth cup.

Praise God, all nations, Praise God, all peoples.
God's love overwhelms us,
And God's truth endures forever. *Halleluyah!*
(Psalm 117)

If our mouths were as filled with song as the sea,
And our tongues with joy as the endless waves,
And our lips with praise as the wide expanse of the heavens;
If our eyes were as radiant as the sun and the moon,
And our hands were spread out like eagles' wings,
And our feet were swift as deer,
Yet we would be unable to thank you,
Our God and God of our ancestors,
For one small measure of the kindness you
have shown to our ancestors and to us.
(from the prayer *Nishmat Kol Chai*)

Think About:

What are some things for which you are grateful? Can you think of an act of kindness that lasts forever?

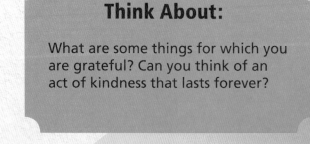

The Fourth Cup

Raise the fourth cup of wine or grape juice and read together the fourth of the four promises:

"I will take you to be my people, and I will be your God." (Exodus 6:7)

Say the blessing:

בָּרוּךְ אַתָּה יְיָ אֱלֹהֵינוּ מֶלֶךְ הָעוֹלָם, בּוֹרֵא פְּרִי הַגָּפֶן.

Baruch Atah Adonai Eloheinu Melech ha'olam, borei p'ri hagafen.

Praised are You, Adonai our God, Ruler of the universe, who creates the fruit of the vine.

Drink from the fourth cup of wine or grape juice.

Nirtzah
Completing the Seder

We have now reached the end of our seder. We hope that the rituals and thoughts that we have offered have been meaningful. We are grateful that our people were freed from Egypt and believe that the best is yet to come.

לְשָׁנָה הַבָּאָה בִּירוּשָׁלַיִם.

L'shanah haba'ah biY'rushalayim!

Next year in Jerusalem!

May the coming year bring freedom, peace, and redemption to Israel and to all humankind.

Uh-oh.

Think About:
What do you hope next year will be like? For you? Your family? The world?

Echad Mi Yodei'a: Who Knows One?

This playful song uses numbers to teach Jewish concepts.

Echad mi yodei'a? Echad ani yodei'a: Echad Eloheinu shebashamayim uva'aretz.

Sh'nayim mi yodei'a? Sh'nayim ani yodei'a: Sh'nei luchot habrit, echad Eloheinu shebashamayim uva'aretz.

Sh'loshah mi yodei'a? Sh'loshah ani yodei'a: Sh'loshah avot, sh'nei luchot habrit, echad Eloheinu shebashamayim uva'aretz.

Arba mi yodei'a? Arba ani yodei'a: Arba imahot, sh'loshah avot, sh'nei luchot habrit, echad Eloheinu shebashamayim uva'aretz.

Chamishah mi yodei'a? Chamishah ani yodei'a: Chamishah chumshei Torah, arba imahot, sh'loshah avot, sh'nei luchot habrit, echad Eloheinu shebashamayim uva'aretz.

Shishah mi yodei'a? Shishah ani yodei'a: Shishah sidrei Mishnah, chamishah chumshei Torah, arba imahot, sh'loshah avot, sh'nei luchot habrit, echad Eloheinu shebashamayim uva'aretz.

Shivah mi yodei'a? Shivah ani yodei'a: Shivah y'mei Shabta, shishah sidrei Mishnah, chamishah chumshei Torah, arba imahot, sh'loshah avot, sh'nei luchot habrit, echad Eloheinu shebashamayim uva'aretz.

Sh'monah mi yodei'a? Sh'monah ani yodei'a: Sh'monah y'mei milah, shivah y'mei Shabta, shishah sidrei Mishnah, chamishah chumshei Torah, arba imahot, sh'loshah avot, sh'nei luchot habrit, echad Eloheinu shebashamayim uva'aretz.

Tishah mi yodei'a? Tishah ani yodei'a: Tishah yarchei leidah, sh'monah y'mei milah, shivah y'mei Shabta, shishah sidrei Mishnah, chamishah chumshei Torah, arba imahot, sh'loshah avot, sh'nei luchot habrit, echad Eloheinu shebashamayim uva'aretz.

Asarah mi yodei'a? Asarah ani yodei'a: Asarah dibraya, tishah yarchei leidah, sh'monah y'mei milah, shivah y'mei Shabta, shishah sidrei Mishnah, chamishah chumshei Torah, arba imahot, sh'loshah avot, sh'nei luchot habrit, echad Eloheinu shebashamayim uva'aretz.

Achad asar mi yodei'a? Achad asar ani yodei'a: Achad asar koch'vaya, asarah dibraya, tishah yarchei leidah, sh'monah y'mei milah, shivah y'mei Shabta, shishah sidrei Mishnah, chamishah chumshei Torah, arba imahot, sh'loshah avot, sh'nei luchot habrit, echad Eloheinu shebashamayim uva'aretz.

Sh'neim asar mi yodei'a? Sh'neim asar ani yodei'a: Sh'neim asar shivtaya, achad asar koch'vaya, asarah dibraya, tishah yarchei leidah, sh'monah y'mei milah, shivah y'mei Shabta, shishah sidrei Mishnah, chamishah chumshei Torah, arba imahot, sh'loshah avot, sh'nei luchot habrit, echad Eloheinu shebashamayim uva'aretz.

Sh'loshah asar mi yodei'a? Sh'loshah asar ani yodei'a: Sh'loshah asar midaya, sh'neim asar shivtaya, achad asar koch'vaya, asarah dibraya, tishah yarchei leidah, sh'monah y'mei milah, shivah y'mei Shabta, shishah sidrei Mishnah, chamishah chumshei Torah, arba imahot, sh'loshah avot, sh'nei luchot habrit, echad Eloheinu shebashamayim uva'aretz.

Who knows one? I know one: One is our God in heaven and on earth.

Who knows two? I know two: Two are the tablets of the law, and one is our God in heaven and on earth.

Who knows three? I know three: Three are the patriarchs, two are the tablets of the law, and one is our God in heaven and on earth.

Four are the matriarchs…

Five are the books of the Torah…

Six are the books of the Mishnah…

Seven are the days of the week…

Eight are the days until circumcision…

Nine are the months of pregnancy…

Ten are the commandments…

Eleven are the stars in Joseph's dream…

Twelve are the tribes of Israel…

Thirteen are the attributes of God…

The Ten Commandments,
Alsace, 19th century

It's hard to count on webbed toes...

when Frog found the afikoman.

Think About:

Complete these sentences:

My favorite part of the seder was…

For next year's seder I hope …

Chad Gadya: One Little Goat

This Aramaic folk song describes Israel's trials with its enemies throughout history. The little goat represents Israel, and the father is God, the Holy One. The two coins, *zuzim,* are the tablets of the law, and the remaining figures are Israel's past enemies: Assyria (the cat), Babylon (the dog), Persia (the stick), Greece (the fire), Rome (the water), the Saracens (the ox), the Crusaders (the butcher), and the Ottoman Turks (the angel of death).

Chad gadya, chad gadya, **dizvan aba bitrei zuzei, chad gadya, chad gadya.**

V'ata shunra, v'achlah l'gadya, **dizvan aba bitrei zuzei, chad gadya, chad gadya.**

V'ata chalba, v'nashach l'shunra, d'achlah l'gadya, **dizvan aba bitrei zuzei, chad gadya, chad gadya.**

V'ata chutra, v'hikah l'chalba, d'nashach l'shunra, d'achlah l'gadya, **dizvan aba bitrei zuzei, chad gadya, chad gadya.**

V'ata nura, v'saraf l'chutra, d'hikah l'chalba, d'nashach l'shunra, d'achlah l'gadya, **dizvan aba bitrei zuzei, chad gadya, chad gadya.**

V'ata maya, v'chavah l'nura, d'saraf l'chutra, d'hikah l'chalba, d'nashach l'shunra, d'achlah l'gadya, **dizvan aba bitrei zuzei, chad gadya, chad gadya.**

V'ata tora, v'shata l'maya, d'chavah l'nura, d'saraf l'chutra, d'hikah l'chalba, d'nashach l'shunra, d'achlah l'gadya, **dizvan aba bitrei zuzei, chad gadya, chad gadya.**

V'ata hashocheit, v'shachat l'tora, d'shata l'maya, d'chavah l'nura, d'saraf l'chutra, d'hikah l'chalba, d'nashach l'shunra, d'achlah l'gadya, **dizvan aba bitrei zuzei, chad gadya, chad gadya.**

V'ata malach hamavet, v'shachat l'shocheit, d'shachat l'tora, d'shata l'maya, d'chavah l'nura, d'saraf l'chutra, d'hikah l'chalba, d'nashach l'shunra, d'achlah l'gadya, **dizvan aba bitrei zuzei, chad gadya, chad gadya.**

V'ata haKadosh Baruch Hu, v'shachat l'malach hamavet, d'shachat l'shocheit, d'shachat l'tora, d'shata l'maya, d'chavah l'nura, d'saraf l'chutra, d'hikah l'chalba, d'nashach l'shunra, d'achlah l'gadya, **dizvan aba bitrei zuzei, chad gadya, chad gadya.**

"Chad Gadya" column
in Castra Center, Haifa

Try This!

As you sing the song, make the sound for each character. For example, when the cat is mentioned, say "meow"; when the dog is mentioned, "bow wow"; and so on.

(You might have to get creative for some of the last ones, like God or the angel of death!)

frog   *frog*

One little goat, one little goat, my father bought for two *zuzim, chad gadya, chad gadya.*

frog

Then came a cat and ate the goat my father bought for two *zuzim, chad gadya, chad gadya.*

Then came a dog and bit the cat that ate the goat my father bought for two *zuzim, chad gadya, chad gadya.*

Then came a stick and hit the dog that bit the cat that ate the goat my father bought for two *zuzim, chad gadya, chad gadya.*

Then came a fire and burned the stick that hit the dog that bit the cat that ate the goat my father bought for two *zuzim, chad gadya, chad gadya.*

Then came water and quenched the fire that burned the stick that hit the dog that bit the cat that ate the goat my father bought for two *zuzim, chad gadya, chad gadya.*

Then came an ox and drank the water that quenched the fire that burned the stick that hit the dog that bit the cat that ate the goat my father bought for two *zuzim, chad gadya, chad gadya.*

Then came a butcher and slaughtered the ox that drank the water that quenched the fire that burned the stick that hit the dog that bit the cat that ate the goat my father bought for two *zuzim, chad gadya, chad gadya.*

Then came the angel of death and killed the butcher that slaughtered the ox that drank the water that quenched the fire that burned the stick that hit the dog that bit the cat that ate the goat my father bought for two *zuzim, chad gadya, chad gadya.*

Then came the Holy Blessed One and destroyed the angel of death that killed the butcher that slaughtered the ox that drank the water that quenched the fire that burned the stick that hit the dog that bit the cat that ate the goat my father bought for two *zuzim, chad gadya, chad gadya.*

Wait! The cat eats the frog? I'm outta here!

Chad Gadya by El Lissitzky, 1919

Answer Key:

Page 15

M C	Miriam's Cup
4 Q	4 Questions
8 D of P	8 Days of Passover
4 C of W	4 Cups of Wine
10 P	10 Plagues
H S	Hillel Sandwich
F C	Frog's Cup

Page 44

GUALPE	Plague
TYPGE	Egypt
EFMDORE	Freedom
TAZHMA	Matzah
CLOTSUS	Locusts
SUFPRCGO	Frog's Cup

Time flies when you have a fun Hopgaddah! I am ready for some Zzzzzz...